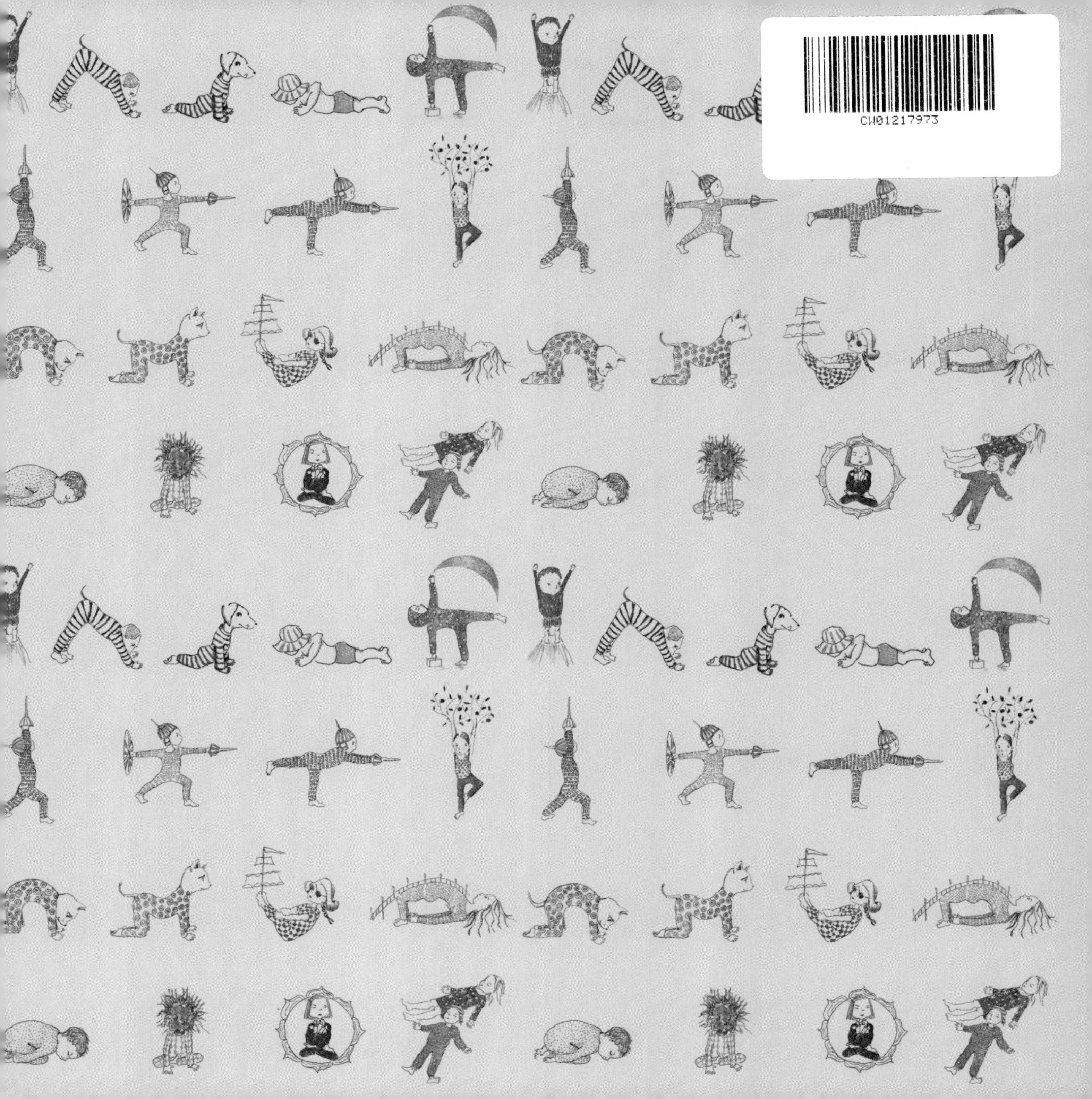

Jack Sharman.

KIDS YOGA

for Ylva and Jack

by Karin Eklund

Copyright © 2017 Karin Eklund

The moral right of the author has been asserted.

Apart from any fair dealing for the purposes of research or private study, or criticism or review, as permitted under the Copyright, Designs and Patents Act 1988, this publication may only be reproduced, stored or transmitted, in any form or by any means, with the prior permission in writing of the publishers, or in the case of reprographic reproduction in accordance with the terms of licences issued by the Copyright Licensing Agency. Enquiries concerning reproduction outside those terms should be sent to the publishers.

Matador
9 Priory Business Park, Wistow Road, Kibworth Beauchamp, Leicestershire. LE8 0RX
Tel: 0116 279 2299 Email: books@troubador.co.uk
Web: www.troubador.co.uk/matador
Twitter: @matadorbooks

ISBN 978 1788033 398

British Library Cataloguing in Publication Data.
A catalogue record for this book is available from the British Library.

Printed and bound in Malta by Gutenberg Press Ltd

Matador is an imprint of Troubador Publishing Ltd

Thanks to my family, without whom this book would not have been possible. And a big thank you to all my teachers and students who continue to inspire me and for all their helpful comments.
A special thanks to Karen Eng, Margaret Deith, Marcus Freeman, Jessica Lack and Natalia Maca.

SAFETY INFORMATION

As with all physical exercise routines these yoga poses should only be attempted with care and attention for the safety of the participants. Let everyone progress at their own pace. Do not try to force yourself or anyone else to move into poses that are uncomfortable in any way.

Everyone's body is different and, while some may be flexible and able to attain all the poses with ease, others may find some poses more of a challenge.

Use common sense and always pay attention to what your body is telling you. You should be able to feel your body and muscles flexing and stretching, but it's not supposed to hurt. If you have any kind of preexisting medical condition you should always seek the advice of a medical professional before attempting any of the poses in this book.

Yoga can be helpful for alleviating the symptoms of many conditions, but that is a specialist subject not covered in this book. The author and the publisher cannot be held responsible for any injury or pain experienced as result of attempting any of the yoga poses suggested in this book.

KIDS YOGA

Welcome to Kids Yoga. How exciting that you have decided to practise yoga and join us on this wonderful journey!

Each yoga pose or asana is inspired by nature and animals. You can try these on your own or with an adult. Let the pictures guide you. Try to imagine what it would be like to be a real lion, a growing tree or a sleeping dormouse. Let your imagination run free. You can even make up your own poses based on the animals and plants in your part of the world.

Usually you would practise yoga in bare feet and comfortable clothes. If you have a yoga mat, roll it out flat. Otherwise just find a clear space on the floor. Grass lawns and sandy beaches also make good surfaces for yoga.

The text explains the name of each pose (in both English and Sanskrit) and how to move into it.

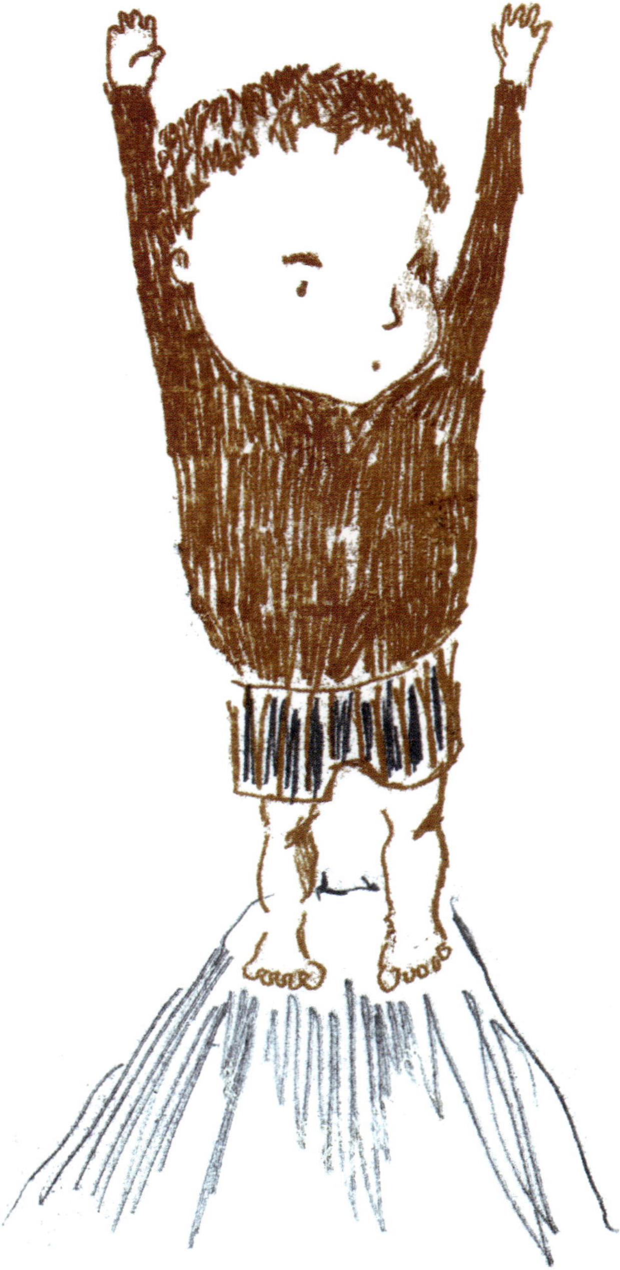

mountain

Tadasana

Like a mountain, stand still, quiet and stable.

Mountain pose is the starting point for all standing poses. Your legs are firmly planted on the ground, heavy and balanced like the base of a high mountain. Your body is tall and strong, and your arms reach up to form the highest peak. If you look down, you will see the Earth way beneath you.

dog
Adho Mukha Svanasana and Urdhva Mukha Svanasana

Stretch like a sleepy dog that's just woken up.

Dogs walk on all fours, so place your four paws on your mat. Lift your tail high while you straighten your arms and legs.

You can walk around or stand still with your heels close to the mat, or wag your tail from side to side. This is Downward-Facing Dog.

Now lower yourself onto the floor to lie flat on your tummy. Slowly straighten your arms and arch your back, drawing the shoulders back and looking up. This is Upward-Facing Dog.

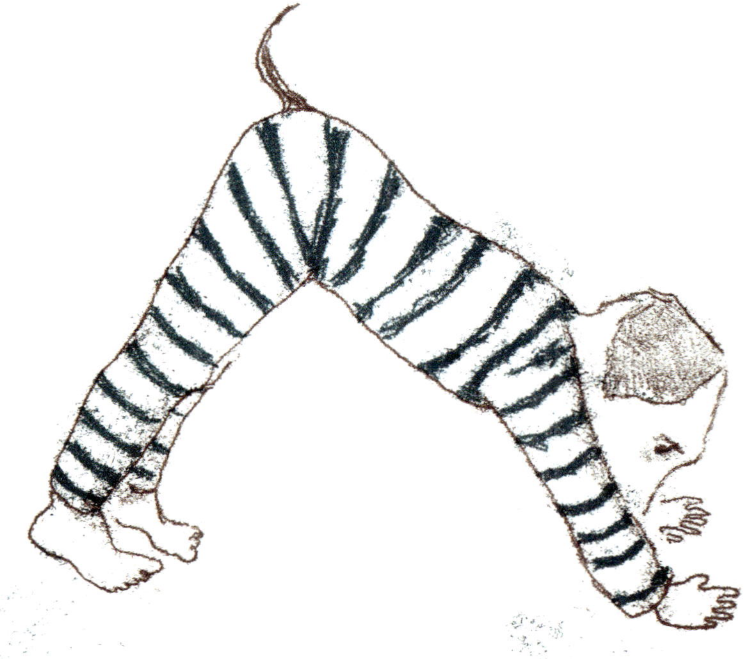

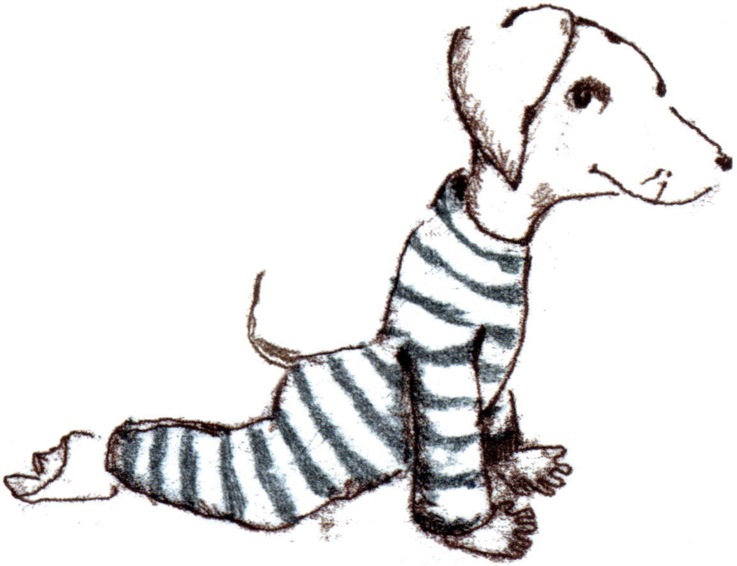

Say 'Good Morning' to the rising Sun.

First, lift your arms high above your head.

Now take a bow, touch the ground, and walk your feet backwards until your body is straight and flat like a piece of wood. This is Plank Position.

Bend your arms so your nose comes close to the floor to smell the Earth before arching your back into an Upward-Facing Dog.

Lift your hips straight up into a Downward-Facing Dog and take five deep breaths, then walk your feet forward to your hands. Straighten your legs, and lift your back. Now move into a standing postition with your arms raised high above your head.

To end the sequence, bring your feet together and your arms down by your sides.

If you repeat the Sun Salute a few times, your body will be warm and stretchy and ready for action.

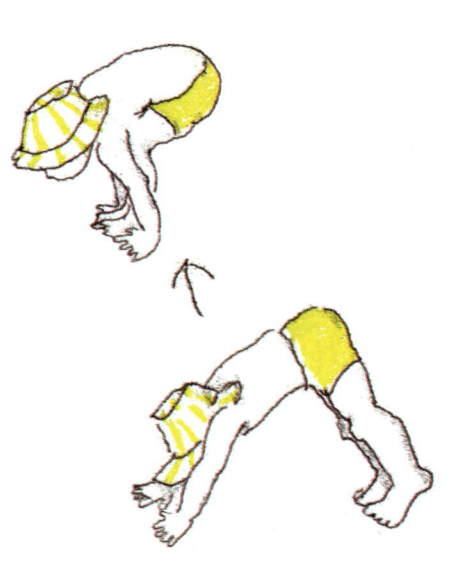

sun salute

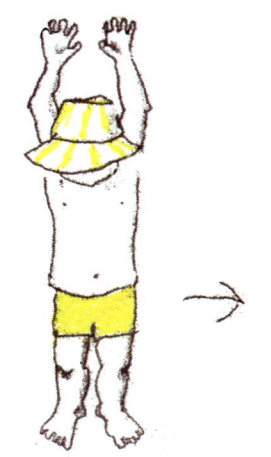

Surya Namaskara

warrior
Virabhadrasana

There are three kinds of warriors, all strong and brave.

Look ahead and stride forward with your legs wide apart. Bend your front leg and keep your back leg straight, toes turned out. Stretch your arms up like you're holding a sword in your hands, pointing it straight up to the sky. This is Warrior 1.

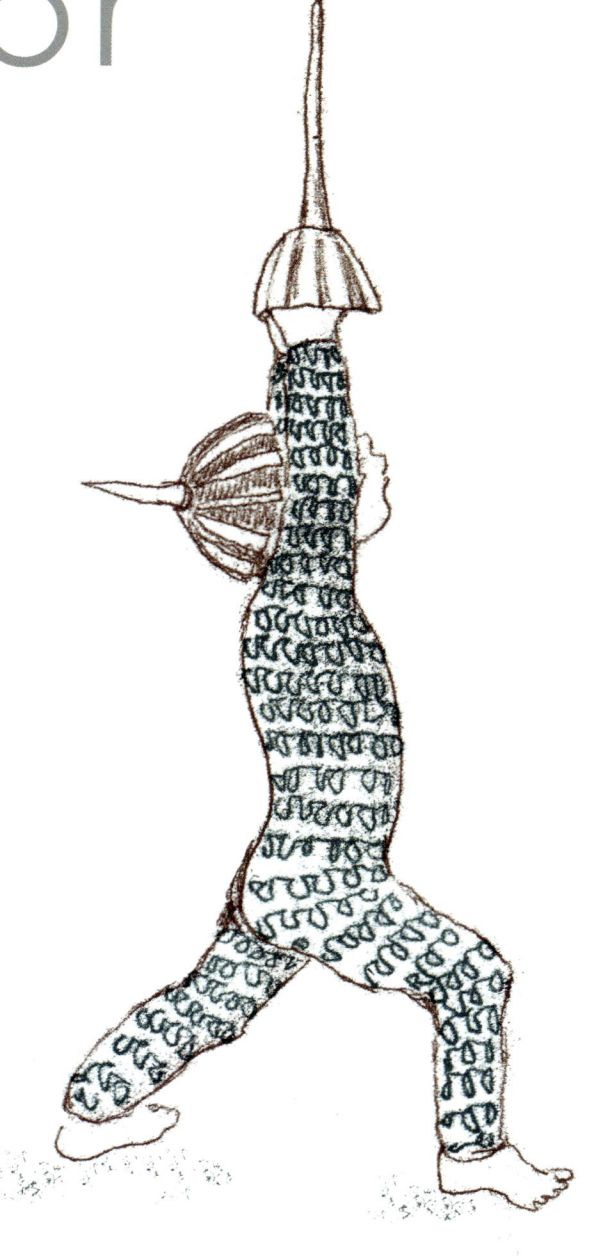

Now open your arms and turn your hips to the side, keeping your front leg bent. Reach out wide, one arm pointing your sword forwards, the other defending your back with your shield. This is Warrior 2.

Try balancing on your front leg, lifting your back leg up to form a straight line with your arm. This combines your strength and balance. Try to hold this position for five breaths.
This is Warrior 3.

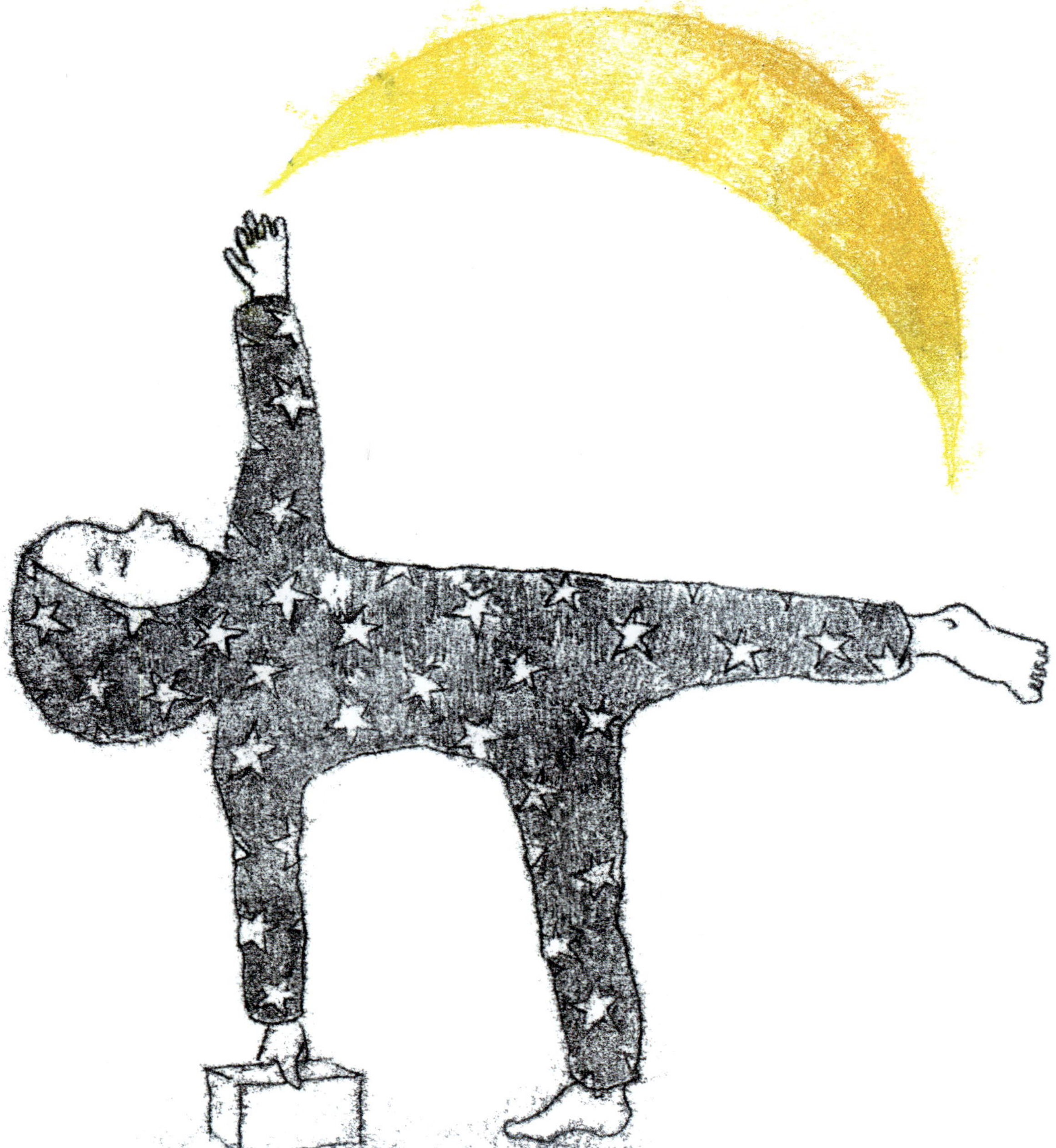

half moon

Ardha Chandrasana

Imagine you are holding up the Moon.

Start by standing on your right leg and placing your right hand on the ground for balance (you can put your hand on a block if it's easier to reach). Lift your left leg up parallel to the ground. Your back is flat as if you are standing against a wall.

The brilliant light from the Moon is shining down on your strong and balanced body.

tree
Vrksasana

Stretch your arms high above your head, like the branches of a tree.

One leg is the trunk with your toes planted into the soil like roots reaching down for water. Your other leg is bent with the foot resting on your inner thigh. You feel rooted, balanced and calm, steadily growing.

Your branches may gently sway in the breeze, but your trunk and roots are always still and firmly grounded.

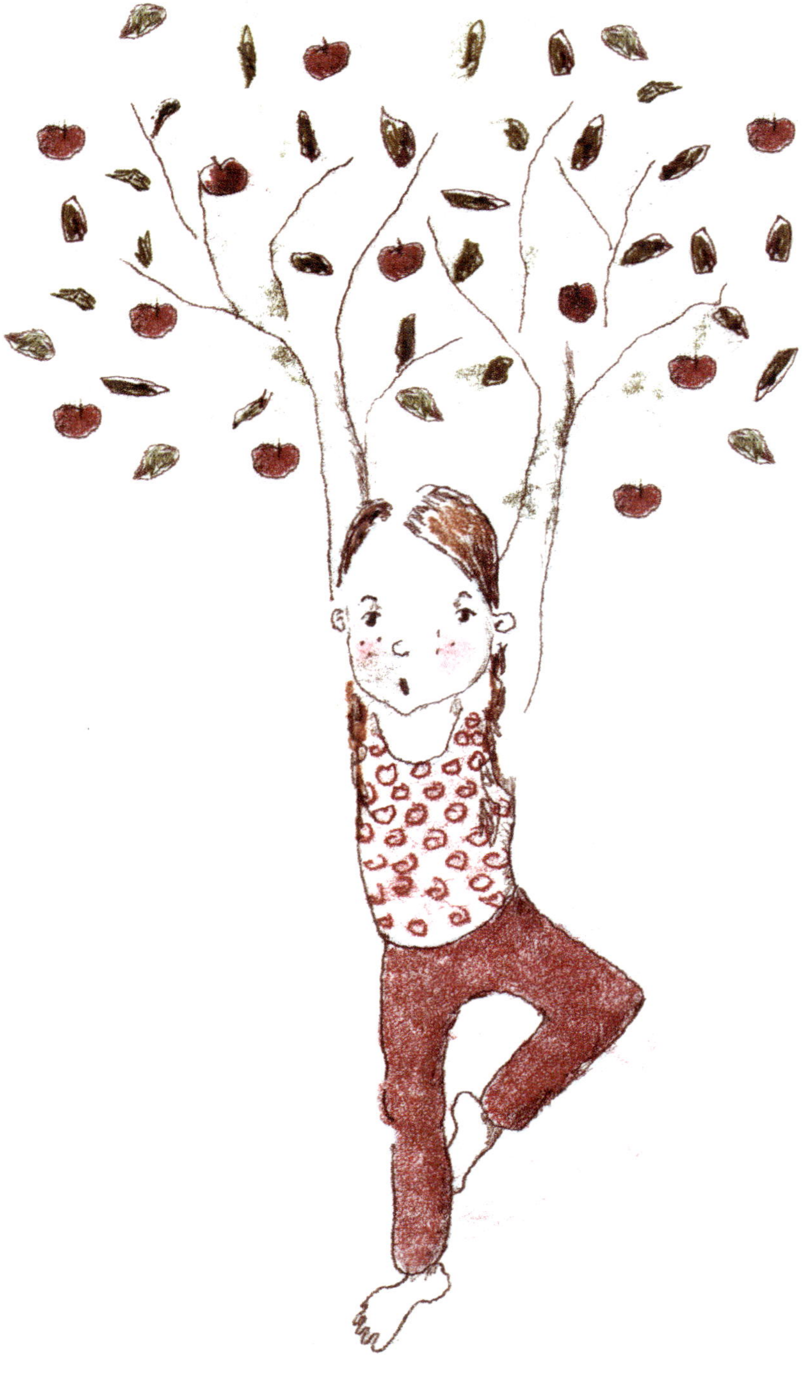

cat

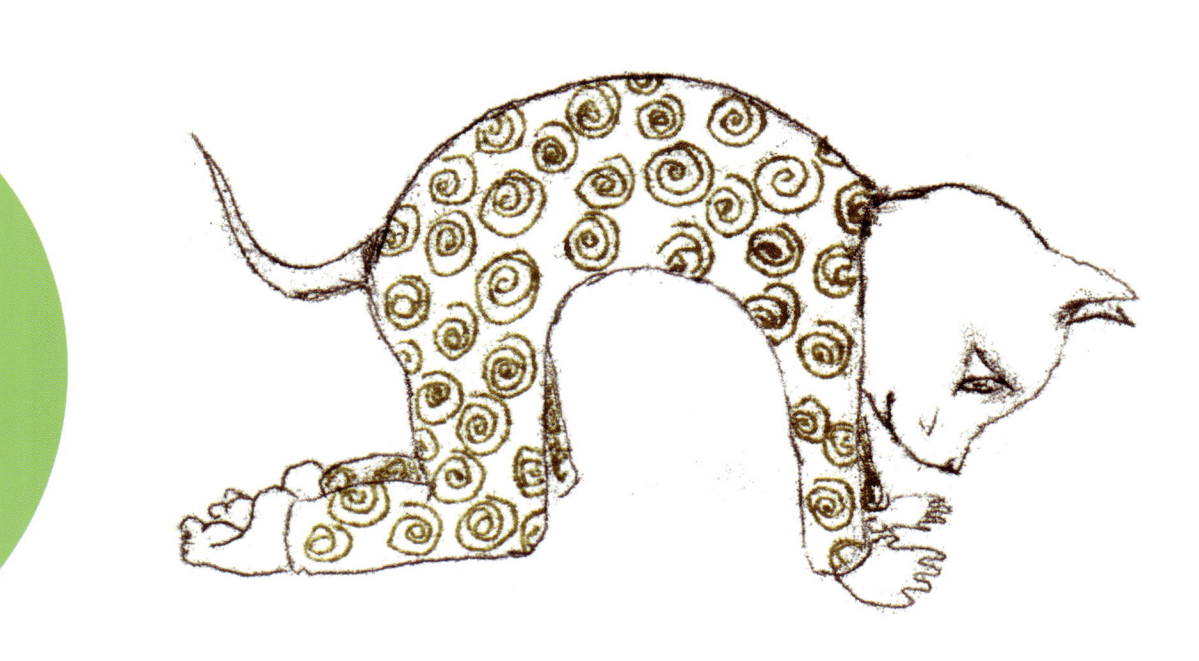

Marjaryasana

Cats are very bendy and jump and climb a lot.

Start as an Angry Cat with the back rounded, fur standing up all over, making you look fierce and dangerous. Your knees should be as wide as your hips, your arms as wide as your shoulders and your head curled in.

The danger has passed. Now you're a Happy Cat, back arched with your tail lifted high, stretching your neck and head up.

Move back and forth between these two cat poses to stretch your back, chest and stomach.

bridge
Setu Bandha Sarvangasana

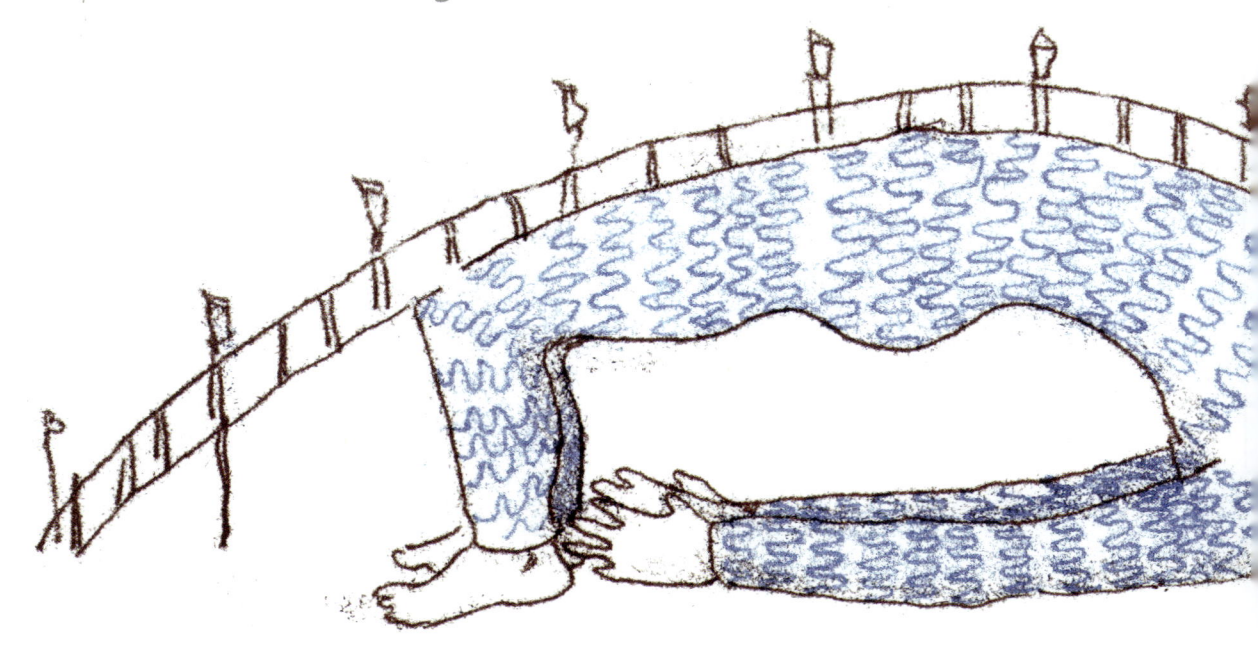

Imagine your body is a bridge arching over a great flowing river.

Lie flat on your back with your knees bent and your feet firmly planted on the floor and slightly apart. Your arms are by your sides, palms facing down. Lift your hips high.

To make your bridge stronger, clasp your hands together behind your back, intertwining your fingers and pressing them into the ground. If your hands will reach, try to take hold of your ankles.

dormouse

Balasana

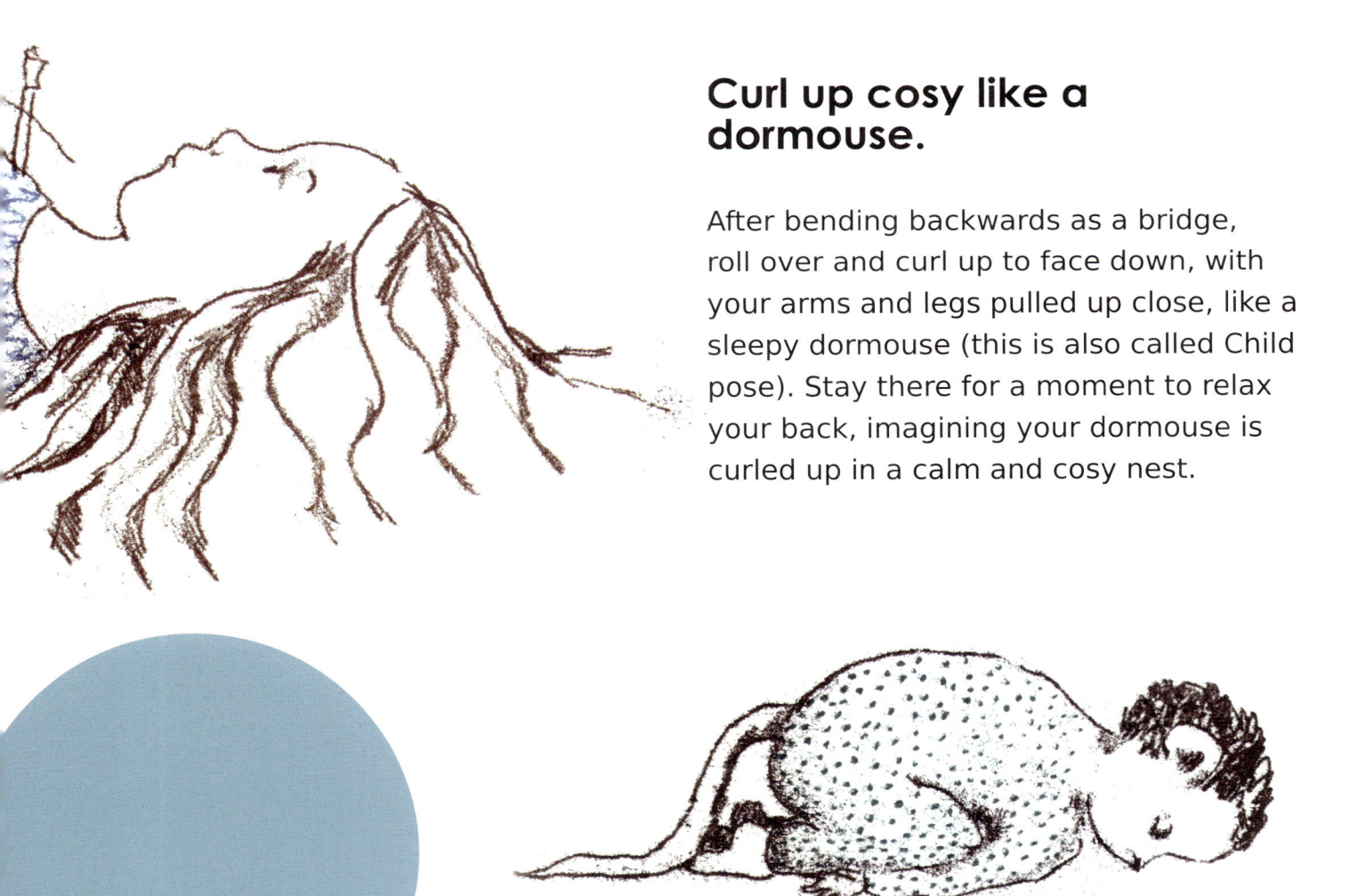

Curl up cosy like a dormouse.

After bending backwards as a bridge, roll over and curl up to face down, with your arms and legs pulled up close, like a sleepy dormouse (this is also called Child pose). Stay there for a moment to relax your back, imagining your dormouse is curled up in a calm and cosy nest.

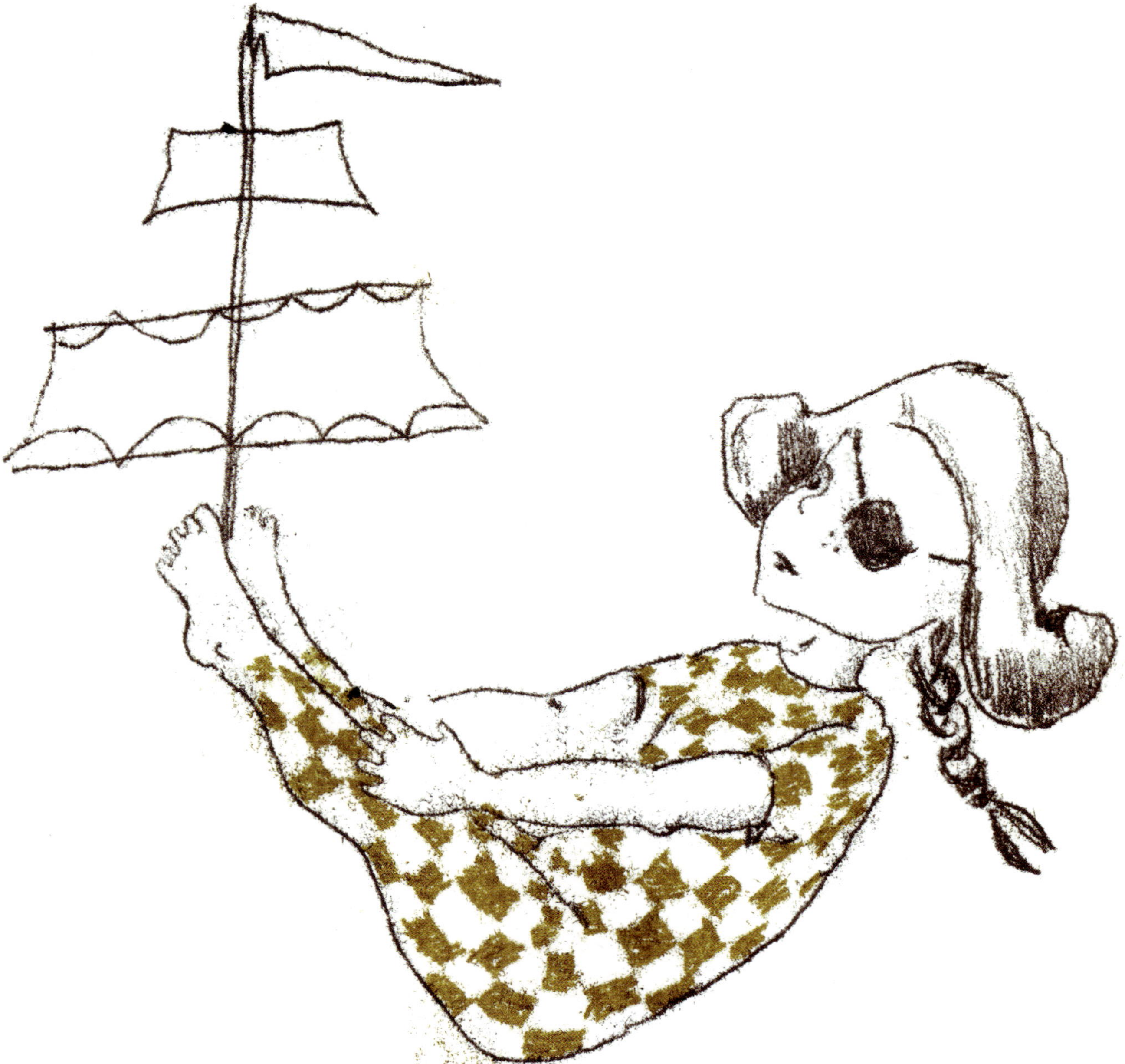

boat
Navasana

Tiny boats or great tall ships – all float calmly on water.

Starting in a sitting position, lift your arms and legs off the floor, making your body into a V-shape like the hull of a boat. Balance on your bottom with your legs, back and head lifted.

The water can be calm and still, or rough with waves riding high and wild. Try steering your boat steadily through the water and holding your balance for five full breaths, in and out.

lion
Simhasana

Roar like a fierce lion.

Sitting with your feet crossed and back straight, give a great roar. This pose inspires courage and strength.

Open your paws and place them on the ground in front of your legs. Stick out your long lion tongue and exhale with a loud roar… Haaaaaaah…

Relax and open your jaws as wide as you can, showing your scary sharp teeth.

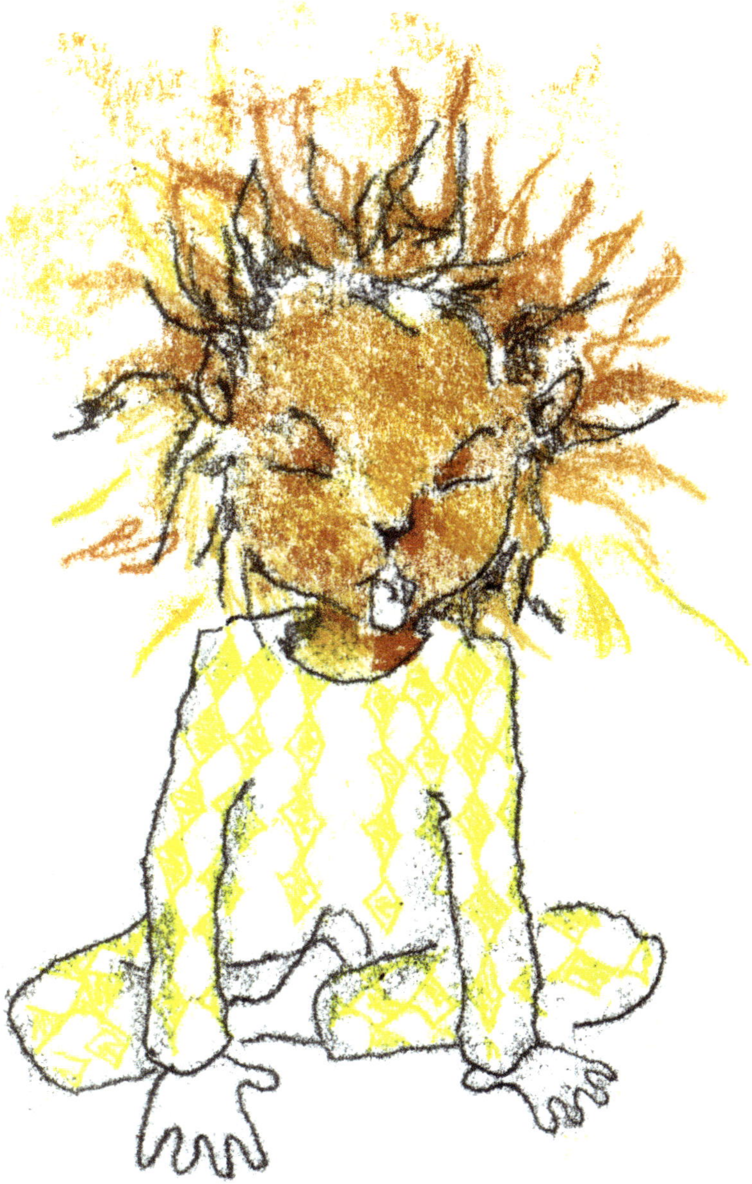

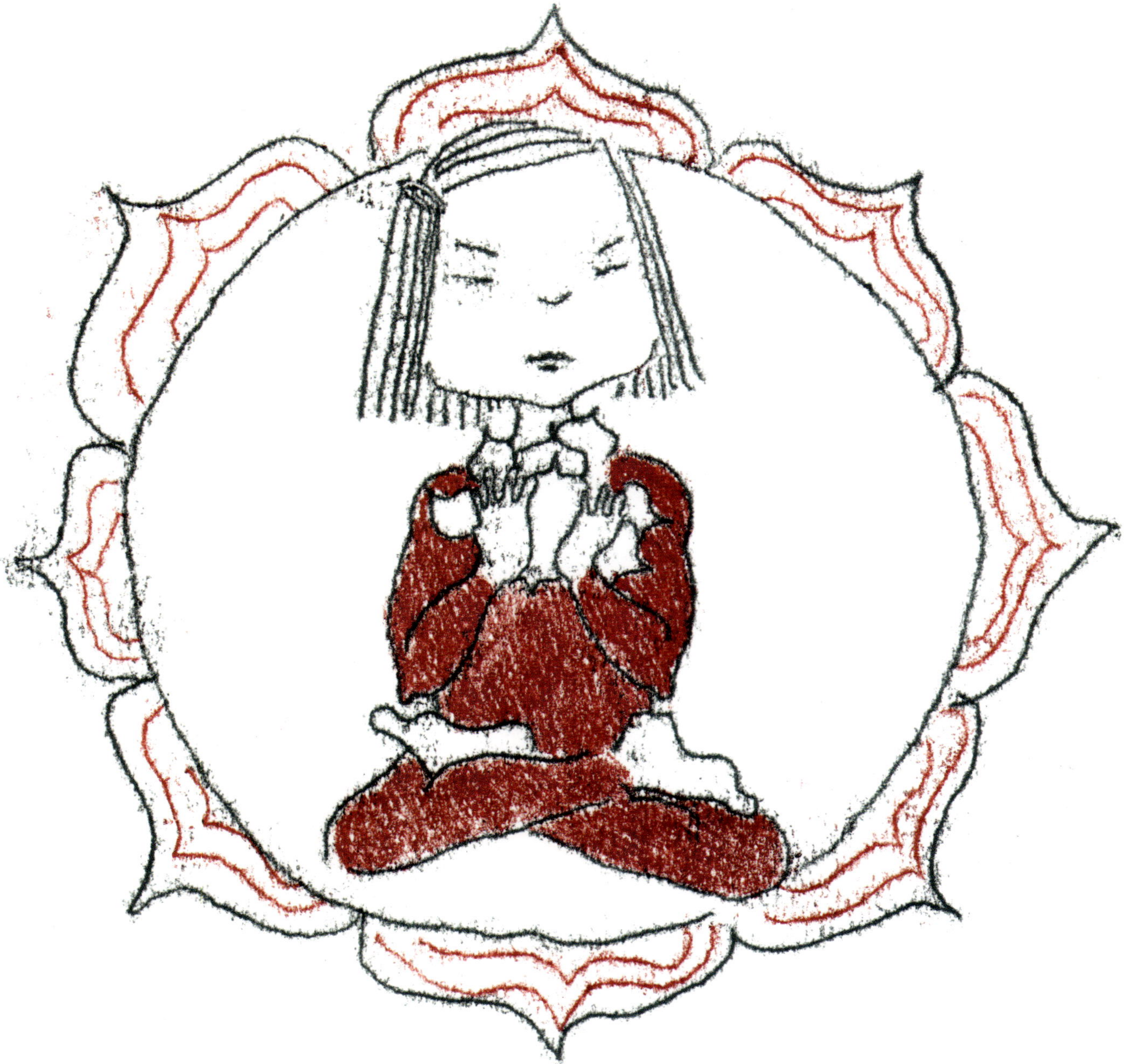

lotus

Padmasana

Blossom like a lotus flower.

The lotus flower is a symbol of beauty, purity and harmony. It rises from murky pond water and blooms as a beautifully clean white flower. This is the traditional pose for meditation.

Cross your legs (or, if you are more flexible, lift your feet so they rest on the opposite thighs). Now straighten your spine and let your wrists meet in front of your chest, spreading your fingers out like the petals of a flower.

Lotus flowers open up when the Sun comes out and close into a bud at night, so now move your hands in a circling motion, looking down at your moving wrists, opening and closing the petals.

sleepy
Savasana

Float away on a cloud.

After your yoga practice, spend a few moments lying down as if you were going to fall asleep. Let all the muscles in your body go soft, sleepy and relaxed. Quietly listen to your breathing. Imagine your yoga mat is floating away, moving gently through the sky, your body floating softly on the clouds.

After a few minutes, finish by sitting upright once again, placing the palms of your hands together in front of your heart. Take a moment to rest, think about something that makes you happy and calm… Namaste.

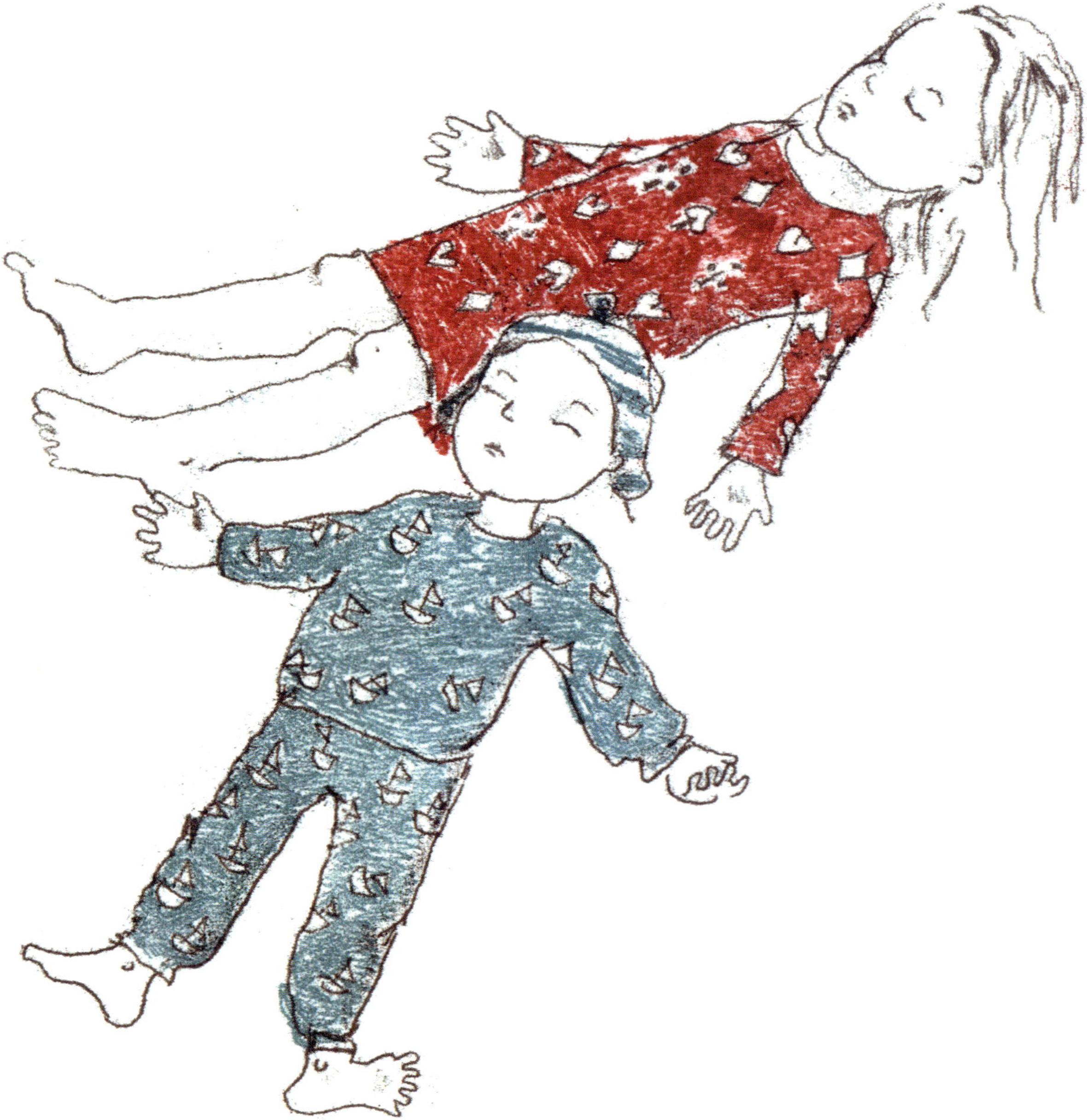

Thank you for practising with us today. I hope you enjoyed it!

There are a lot more yoga poses to explore in the future, but this sequence is a good start, and if you practise a lot you will find the more advanced poses much easier.

As you can see, the sequence moves through a series of active standing poses which strengthen and stimulate body and mind. They then move into calmer sitting poses, finally coming to a restful state. Now you're calm, grounded and ready for anything – play, study or just relaxing.

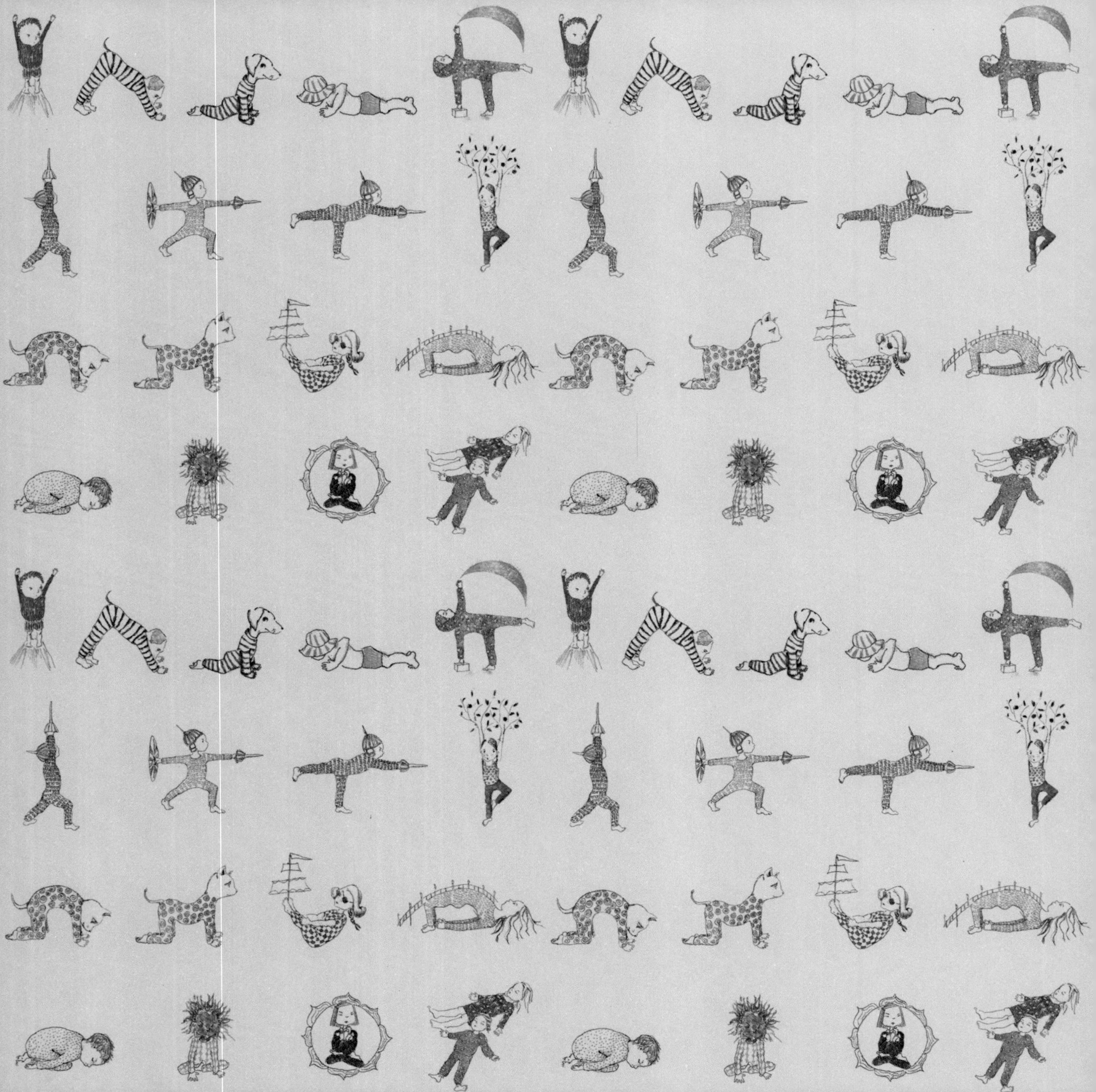